Parchment
Craft

Parchment Craft

Gwen Morris

Kangaroo Press

First published in Australia in 1998 by Kangaroo Press
an imprint of Simon & Schuster Australia
20 Barcoo Street, East Roseville NSW 2069

A Viacom Company
Sydney New York London Toronto Tokyo Singapore

National Library of Australia
Cataloguing-in-Publication data

Morris, Gwen, 1935–.
Parchment craft.

Includes index.
ISBN 0 86417 949 9.

1. Parchment. 2. Paperwork. 3. Greeting cards. I. Title.

745.54

Internal design: Anne Savage
Photography: John de Rooy

Set in Goudy OlSt BT 10/12
Calligraph421 BT

Printed in Hong Kong through Colorcraft Ltd

Contents

Introduction

In ancient times, papyrus was most commonly used for writing and painting, though animal skins were sometimes used. During the second century BC, in Bergama in Turkey, a special treatment of animal skins was developed which made them more suitable for the purpose. These skins were called parchment.

The art of decorating parchment began in the Spanish monasteries in the Middle Ages. The monks discovered that the parchment could be easily embossed and perforated to produce lacy designs. Today, 'parchment' is paper specially treated so that it becomes opaque when embossed, and stays firm when perforated and cut in lacy patterns.

My father taught me how to emboss drawing paper, and the technique has always fascinated me. I was delighted when I discovered that parchment paper was now readily available. It was so easy to work with and very adaptable to a wide range of designs. When I looked for books on the craft, however, I noted that all the designs were decorative and stylised and featured European or American flora and fauna.

Why are we so taken with a cute fluffy bunny on a card? Why not a cuddly koala or a bilby? Probably because we are so accustomed to seeing 'foreign' flora and fauna on cards and in books. Too often in practising traditional European crafts we tend to follow European tradition in subject matter, not adapting Australian themes.

Cards always bring greetings, whether it's for a special occasion or just to say Hi! A card which you have created makes greeting very personal and can give the receiver great pleasure.

My aim in writing this book is twofold—firstly to show readers that as parchment craft is so easy, and does not require expensive equipment, they too can make their own cards, and secondly to promote and inspire the incorporation of Australian wildlife into the designs.

In this book, I have chosen eighteen subjects, both well known ones such as the kangaroo and flannel flower, and lesser known ones such as the cocky-apple, and have used several techniques to demonstrate how parchment craft can be adapted to Australian flora and fauna designs. I doubt that there is any Australian theme that cannot be used in parchment craft (in my folder I have at least one hundred designs).

Since parchment craft is really just beginning to be known in Australia I have included instructions on how to make the cards, as well as some tips on how to avoid spoiling your creation.

Any craft should be enjoyable and readily accessible to all. Though it is important to have suitable equipment, it is not essential to buy expensive specialised equipment, so I include hints on both what is available and some suitable substitutes.

For painting mediums, a wide variety of felt pens, inks and paints may be used, but remember that non-permanent inks may smudge in the presence of any moisture. Therefore, for children I do recommend that you provide permanent paints and inks.

People often think at first that the whitening of the paper is coming from the embossing tool. It is important to remember that the paper itself becomes white as pressure is applied to it. If you remember this basic rule you will find creating the illusion of depth and shade and light much easier to achieve. You will also become aware of the pressure you are applying and so will be less likely to perforate the paper.

I have not suggested verses or greetings for the inserts, as I find most people want to include their own personal message. May I suggest that when you make cards on commission you only include greetings if your handwriting is very neat; you could also use greeting stamps.

The colours I have used are my personal preference—pastel shades are no more correct than bright colours and vice versa. I prefer to show detail by using degrees of paper whitening and adding background colour, as in the koala design, but some subjects, such as the kangaroo at sunset and the Art Nouveau honeyeater, demand colour.

Equipment & Hints

Paper

It is essential to use the correct parchment paper available from craft shops. When working with the paper ensure that your hands are clean and dry. I use the A4 size in 140 gsm weight.

Embossing tools

A number of special embossing tools are available, although substitute tools, e.g. an empty biro, may be used. The biro must be free of all ink or your work will be spoiled. It is essential that the work surface of any substitute tool is absolutely smooth or your work will be damaged. Large areas can be embossed using the round end of the handle of the embossing tool.

Embossing pad

A pad under the work is necessary when embossing and perforating. The special embossing pads give the best result. A felt pad or a mouse pad may be used, but beware of the grain of the fabric cover of the mouse pad—the embossing tool tends follow the grain. Some mouse pads are not thick enough to allow one to perforate without risking damage to the fine points of the perforating tools.

Perforating tools

Special perforating tools are available at craft shops. The most commonly used are the one-, two- and four-pointed tools. A fine sharp needle may be used as a substitute.

Craft knife

Used for cutting the sheets of parchment paper to the required card size. Use against a steel ruler for a precise edge.

Scissors

The scissors used for making picot and other decorative edges must have short curves and fine points. Special scissors are available which require a special technique to use. However, high quality embroidery scissors may also be used. Insert the tip of a blade about one millimetre into the small perforated hole, very slightly rotate the scissors towards the left and close the points. This method of cutting produces the 'picot' effect in the lace patterns.

There is also a range of scissors called 'Paper Edgers' for trimming the edges of cards or the inserts.

Colour mediums

❖ *Ink* It is safer to use waterproof inks. White, silver and gold ink are most commonly used. Inks will thicken if left open when not in use.

❖ *Oil pastels* Apply the pastel in stripes. An even spread and easy blending is obtained using a drop of white spirit or lighter fluid on a paper towel. Small areas may be blended using a cotton bud.

❖ *Permanent overhead projector pens* These are really only suitable for outlining. They give a streaky appearance if used to colour in large areas.

❖ *Felt pens* Good quality felt pens can be used for small areas. Test them on a parchment scrap first, as some rub off the paper when dry.

❖ *Paints* Some brands of fabric paint, not fabric dyes, can be used on parchment. Always use the 'dry brush' technique as excess moisture will damage the paper.

❖ *Drawing inks* Good quality drawing inks can be used for outlining and colouring. When colouring with ink and brush, remove excess ink from the brush as too much moisture tends to damage the paper.

Miscellaneous

❖ *Chalk pencil* For marking lines, which can readily be removed by the special eraser obtainable from good craft shops. Other erasers may mark the paper. When erasing rub very gently, always with the paper on a smooth, firm surface or it will tend to emboss.

❖ *School ruler* A roller-ruler makes lattice work easier. A cutting slide ruler allows more accurate trimming of edges.

❖ *Pens* Mapping or drawing pens are suitable.

❖ *Paintbrushes* Use fine sable hair or Taklon brushes. You'll have your favourite size, generally 00 to 2 in the range.

❖ *Inserts* Any type of coloured paper can be used for the inserts, remembering that the colour of the insert must enhance the design. The colour of the insert will change the colours of the design to some extent, so experiment. The inserts may be sewn in place using one of several types of threads, e.g. metallic thread, fine crochet cotton. Fine ribbon can also be used to hold in an insert. A glue line will unfortunately be very obvious through parchment paper.

Techniques

As parchment paper is sold as sheets, not readily cut cards, firstly decide what size card you want and cut to size with a sharp craft knife. Remember you only trace on one half of the card as the other half is folded to become the back of the card, so take this into account when cutting your card to size. Mark the fold line with the chalk pencil. Do not fold the card at this stage. When you've selected your design and its placement on the card, secure the parchment onto the pattern using small cylinders of sticky paper, sticky side out. This prevents slipping while you're working. Do not place the sticky paper over any part of the design.

If an outline is part of the design, trace the outline onto the card using the desired colour of ink or paint. Practice is needed to obtain an even fine line using paint. Unless otherwise stated, all tracing is done on the upper side of the card.

Some designs do not require an outline, e.g. the cocky-apple. These may be produced in two ways. If pale delicate shades are wanted, draw the design lightly in chalk pencil onto the card. Remove the card from the design, turn it over and apply the colour to the design on the back of the card. If more vibrant colours are required, e.g. the blue wren, secure the card over the design and copy the design in the colours.

Where the parchment paper is embossed it becomes opaque white. Embossing is done with an embossing tool using gentle pressure to avoid splitting the paper. The illusion of shading is obtained by varying the pressure on the tool.

If you emboss directly on a colour the colour remains strongly visible on the top surface of the parchment, but the embossed area shows white on the under side. When a colour is embossed from the under side of the colour, it lightens. The degree of lightening depends on the depth of the colour. Unless stated otherwise, all embossing is done from the under side of the card.

Lacy patterns are produced by perforating the paper with a perforating tool. Perforation is always done from the upper side. Wherever a design includes perforation, I suggest you photocopy the design from the book and work from the photocopied design to perforate the pattern.

Applying small cylinders of sticky paper to secure the card to the pattern.

Tracing the design onto the card in the desired coloured ink or paint. The outline is part of this design.

An outline is not part of this design, and only pale shades are wanted. Trace the design on the card in chalk pencil. Turn card over and apply colour to underside of the design.

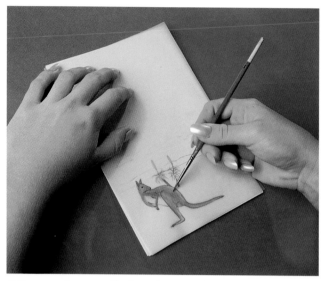

Where a design calls for vibrant colours, secure the card over the pattern and colour each area directly on the upper side of the card.

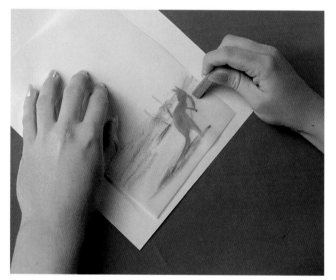

Apply oil pastels in stripes to the under side of the pattern.

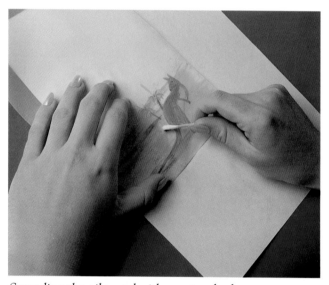

Spreading the oil pastel with a cotton bud.

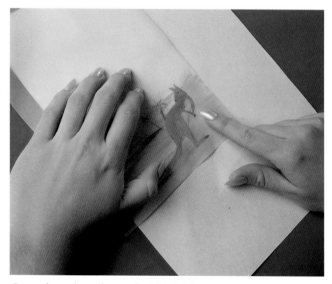

Spreading the oil pastel with the finger.

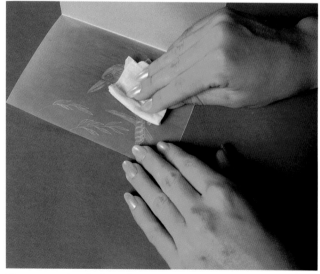

Even spreads of colour from oil pastels is obtained using a drop of white spirit or lighter fluid on soft paper towel or tissue.

Colour remains unchanged when you emboss over it, but the paper shows white on the other side. When this characteristic of the paper is a feature of the design, after you trace the design turn the paper over, apply any colour and carefully emboss the design from the underside.

Note here that the leaves on the under side of the parchment (from which the embossing is done) are solid green, but on the front of the card, the white flowers are clearly visible in front of the leaves.

When a colour is embossed from the under side, it becomes lighter. The degree of lightening depends on the colour.

If you wish to emboss letters you will find it easier to follow the outline of the letter and then fill in.

To work the perforations, secure the card to the design and place on the embossing pad. The tool is held at right angles to the parchment paper and the prongs pushed through.

Hold the scissors vertically when perforating. Insert the tips about one millimetre into the small perforated holes; very slightly rotate the scissors towards the left and close the points. Cutting this way produces the 'picot' effect in the lace patterns.

Picot and lace patterns

Fold the insert and lay it inside the card. Attach a length of ribbon just to the left of the fold, with a small spot of glue. Bring the ribbon onto the front of the card and tie.

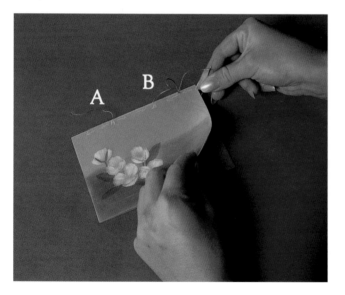

Attaching an insert with glue, small beads of a good quality clear-drying glue are applied to the fold of the insert. The insert is then carefully positioned inside the card.

Attaching an insert with metallic thread: Place the insert inside the card. Use a needle to perforate the card at points A and B. From outside the card, pass the needle and thread through A, along the inside of the insert, around the end of the card and insert the needle in through A again. Take. the thread along the inside of the insert and out through B, round the end of the card and out through B again. Tie the ends.

Lettering

I have included words of greeting on very few of the cards. Instead I have supplied samples of the alphabet in several styles of decorative lettering, from which you can write your own greetings.

ABCDEFGHIJKLM

NOPQRSTUVWXYZ

abcdefghijklmnopqrstuvwxyz

abcdefghijklmnopqrstuvwxyz

abcdefghijklmnopqrstuvwxyz

abcdefghijklmnopqrstuvwxyz

The Designs

Note: Each design is drawn to fit on half an A4 parchment paper sheet.

Kookaburra

Illustrated opposite

Tracing The whole design is traced in white drawing ink.

Embossing
Bird: Emboss using the end of the handle. The pattern on the tail and highlights on the wings are embossed slightly more heavily.
Tree: Branch is lightly embossed, highlights more heavily.

Finishing off Add coloured insert.

OPPOSITE: *Kookaburra, Koala (page 16) and Art Nouveau Nightjar (page 17)*

Koala

Illustrated on page 14

Tracing The whole design is traced in white drawing ink.

Painting On the under side apply oil pastel in the same colour as the insert.

Embossing
Koala: Emboss along the line of the fur pattern.
Tree: Lightly emboss trunk, branch and leaves.

Finishing off Add coloured insert.

Art Nouveau Nightjar

Illustrated on page 14

Tracing

Outlines: Bird, leaves and branches are traced in brown permanent overhead projector pen, though any colour may be used.

Feather patterns: White drawing ink.

Painting On the upper side.

Bird: Beak and centre of eye painted with brown overhead projector pen.

Leaves: Painted in leaf green and a brown-green.

Working on the under side.

Bird: The outer eye is painted with the same brown pen as the centre of the eye.

Embossing The whole bird is lightly embossed with feather patterns being more heavily embossed.

Perforation

Bird: Perforations follow the pattern.

Background: Perforate around the edges of the cut-out areas using a one-prong tool or needle. If perforations are close enough the cut-away will easily pull out. Snip any resistance with scissors as the paper will tear easily.

Finishing off Add coloured insert to coordinate with the tracing colour.

Rock Sprengelia

Illustrated opposite

Tracing

Flowers: Trace in white drawing ink, or gold ink if you prefer.

Border: Trace in white drawing ink, or gold ink if you prefer.

Painting

Flowers: Paint the centres in gold fabric paint.

Leaves: Leaf green fabric paint.

Border: Dot in the centres of border patterns in gold fabric paint.

Embossing

Flowers: Work from tip of each petal toward the centre. Lessen the pressure on the tool towards the centre.

Perforation Secure the card over the design and then perforate the border following the pattern.

Finishing off Add coloured insert.

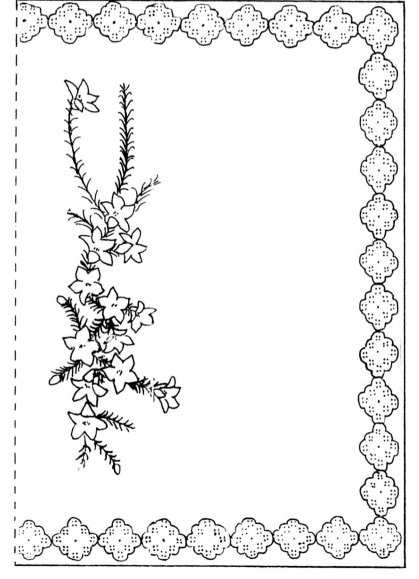

OPPOSITE: *Rock Sprengelia, Flannel Flower (page 20) and Swamp Lilies (page 21)*

Flannel Flower

Illustrated on page 18

Tracing
Flower: The flowers and bud are outlined in white ink.
Border: The dots between the perforations.

Painting Work on the upper side.
Flowers: The centres are painted with a pale gold ink.
Leaves: The leaves are coloured using a leaf-green.

Embossing All petals are embossed working from the tip towards the centre. Lessen the pressure on the embossing tool towards the centre, to give the illusion of depth.

Perforation Secure the card over the design; perforate the border following the pattern.

Finishing off Add an insert.

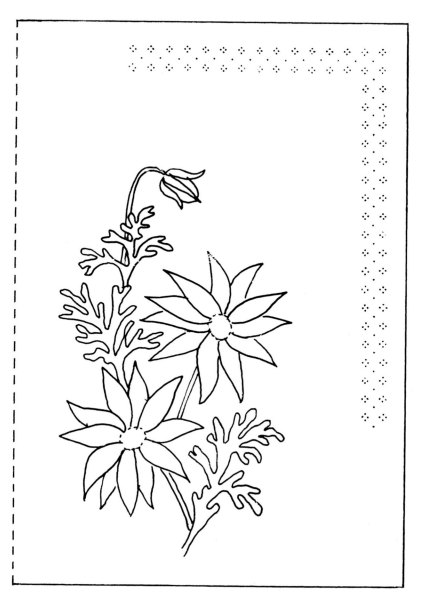

Swamp Lilies

Illustrated on page 18

Tracing Flowers are traced in white drawing ink.

Painting Working on the upper side.
Flower centres: Gold fabric paint.
Sepals and stalks: Leaf green.
Leaves: Leaf green.

Working on the under side.
Water: Turn the card over and apply stripes of colour using mid-blue and mid-green oil pastels. The colours are blended together.

Embossing
Working on the upper side.
Flowers: Open petals.

Working on the under side.
Flowers: Unopened flower and turn-backs on the petals.
Water: Lightly emboss a few highlights.

White Fingers

Illustrated on page opposite

Tracing The flowers, leaves and border are traced in white drawing ink.

Embossing

Flowers: Work from the tips of the petals towards the centre. Lessen the pressure on the tool towards the centre.

Stems: Work along the direction of the stem line.

Leaves: Work from the tip towards the base, to show the natural grain of the leaves.

Border: Work from the apex of the triangle towards the base.

Perforation Secure the card on the design and perforate border pattern.

Finishing off Add a coloured insert.

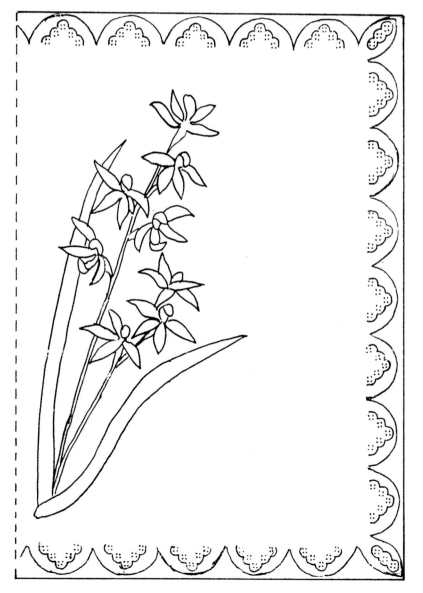

OPPOSITE: *White fingers, Blue Wren (page 24) and Cocky-apple (page 25)*

Blue Wren

Illustrated on page 22

Tracing Borders are traced in white drawing ink.

Painting
Working on the upper side.
Bird: Using the photograph as a guide and following the pattern, add in light blue A, and royal blue B, with a touch of black to the breast. Add black as shown on pattern.

Working on the under side.
Tail: Light blue A and add shading at B.
Wings: Light brown as shown on pattern, adding in highlights in mid-brown, C.
Legs: Mid-brown, C.
Branch: Dark brown.
Leaves: Olive-green.

Embossing All done from the under side.
Bird: Whole body is lightly embossed using end of tool handle.
Border: Emboss with the small tool.

Perforation All done, as shown in pattern, from the upper side.

Finishing off Add a colour insert to enhance the design.

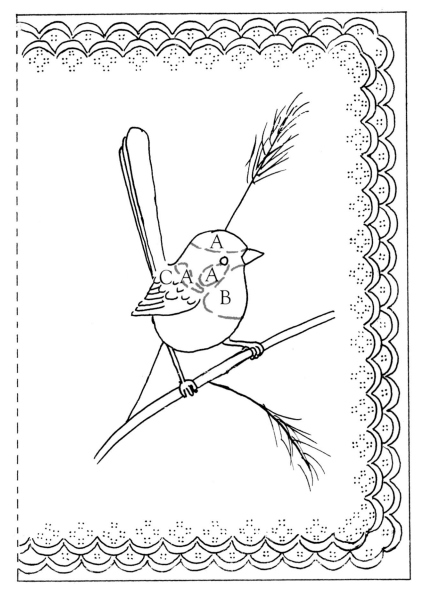

Cocky-apple

Illustrated on page 22

Tracing Outline the design lightly in chalk pencil.

Painting
Work on the under side
Flowers: Pink oil pastel to the base of the flowers, paint sepals pale green.
Leaves: Mid-green paint.
Stalks: Fine mid to light brown paint.

Embossing Using a fine embossing tool and a needle, emboss the fluffy stamen and buds from this side.

Finishing off The edges may be trimmed with Paper Edgers. Add a coloured insert.

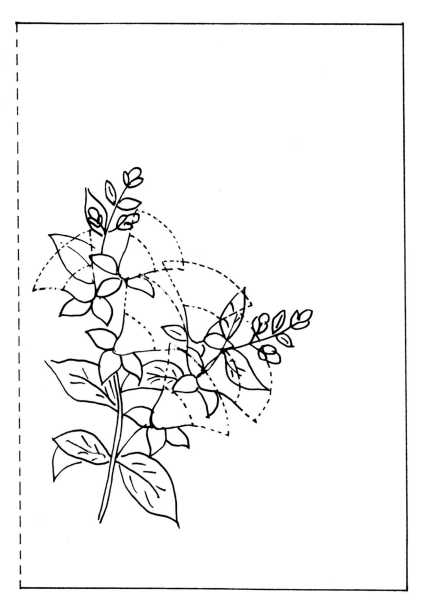

Art Nouveau Autumn Scene

Illustrated opposite

Tracing The outlines are traced with a brown permanent overhead projector pen.

Painting Working on the upper side, following the photograph opposite.
Trees: Vibrant felt pen colours in autumn shades.
Bushes: Bushes are coloured to balance the trees.
Landscape: Area A in dark brown felt pen.
Working on the under side.
Landscape: B in the same dark brown as A.
C in mid brown felt pen.
D in fawn felt pen.

Perforation Secure the card on the design and perforate directly on the design.
Trees: Perforate the patterned area using a two- or four-point tool as shown on the pattern.
Cut-away areas: Perforate around the edge of the area with a one-point tool or a needle. The cut-away will easily pull out if the perforations are close enough. Snip any area that resists or the paper will tear.
Bushes: Perforate as shown in the pattern.

Embossing The sky is lightly embossed, with the edges of the clouds highlighted by heavier embossing.

Finishing off Add a coloured insert.

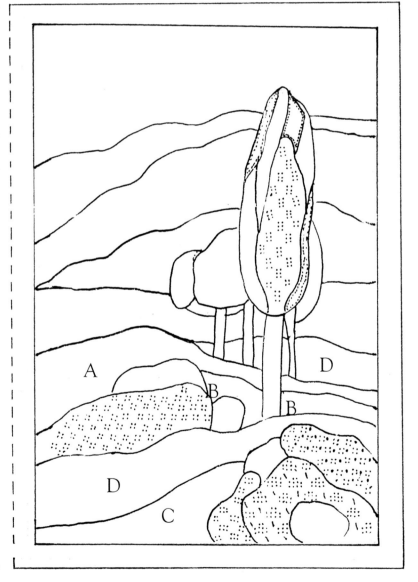

OPPOSITE: *Art Nouveau Autumn Scene, Brolgas (page 28) and Rocky Headland (page 29)*

Brolgas

Illustrated on page 26

Tracing The birds are traced using a permanent black overhead projector pen. The wings are shaded with black fabric paint.

Embossing Working on the upper side.
Birds: The shaded areas on the wings of the bird on the left are embossed from this side to create the illusion of depth.

Working on the under side.
Landscape: The reeds and grass are embossed using the fine embossing tool, while the hills and clouds are lightly embossed with the end of the embossing tool handle.

Finishing off Add a coloured insert.

Rocky Headland

Illustrated on page 26

Tracing The design is traced in brown permanent overhead projector pen.

Painting Work on the under side, using fabric paints.
River: A dull mid-blue.
Sand: Light fawn.
Rocks: Light brown.
Bushes: Mid-green.
Sky: Light blue.

Embossing
Clouds: Lightly embossed.

Perforation The card is secured on the design and directly perforated.
Rocks: Use two- or four-point tool on patterned areas.
Cut-aways: Perforate around edge using one-point tool or needle. If perforations are close enough the area will readily pull away. Snip any resistance with scissors or the paper will readily tear.

Finishing off Add a colour insert which enhances the colours used.

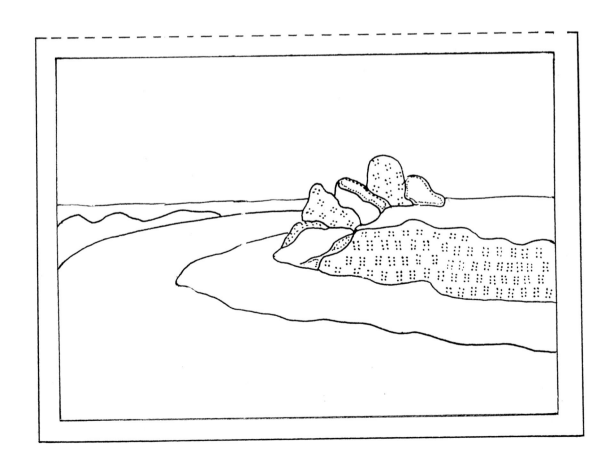

Art Nouveau Honeyeater

Illustrated opposite

Tracing
Bird: Body outline, large wing feathers are traced in black drawing ink. Back feathers are traced in white drawing ink.
Leaves, branches: Black drawing ink.
The design outline may be done in any colour.
Background: Connecting bars traced in white drawing ink.

Painting Work on the under side
Leaves: Olive-green fabric paint.
Branches: Mid brown fabric paint.

Embossing
Bird: Head and tail are moderately heavily embossed, and the body lightly embossed, with the end of the handle of the embossing tool.

Perforation
After embossing the card was secured over the design and the patterns were perforated.
Bird: Work the wing, body and tail patterns using a four-point tool. Closely perforate around the edge of the cut-away areas, using a one-point tool or needle.
Background: Perforate around the borders of the cut-out areas, keeping close to the tracing lines. If the perforations are close enough, the cut-away will pull out easily.

Note: If there is any resistance, snip the holding band with scissors as the paper will easily tear.

Finishing off Add a coloured insert which coordinates with the outline.

OPPOSITE: *Art Nouveau Honeyeater, Gum Blossom (page 32) and Rock Isotome (page 33)*

Gum Blossom

Illustrated on page 30

Tracing Trace blossom, leaves. nuts and stalks in gold ink.

Painting Working on the upper side
Blossoms: Deep pink fabric paint, adding pollen dots in gold ink applied after the paint has dried. The centres are pale green.
Nuts: Gold fabric paint with a touch of brown. The 'cap' line is added in gold ink after the paint has dried.
Leaves: Mid-green paint.
Stalks: Same paint as nuts.

Working on the under side.
Corner pattern: Use the same pink as for the blossoms.

Embossing Blossoms, nuts and floral pattern in corners.

Perforation Secure the card on the design and directly perforate the corner patterns.

Finishing off Add insert and ribbon.

Rock Isotome

Illustrated on page 30

Tracing

Flowers: Traced in white drawing ink, but any colour may be used. Gold or silver are attractive.

Border: Traced in white drawing ink, but any colour may be used.

Oval and circle: Traced in gold.

Painting Turn the card face down and colour the whole area outside the oval with oil pastel. I used an apricot shade. The area within the circle was coloured by blending a cream coloured oil pastel with the apricot.

Embossing

Flowers: Work from tip of petals towards the centre, lessening pressure on the tool towards the centre. Emboss the trumpet part of the flower in lines following the outline, lessening pressure at either end.

Calyx: Work from the tips towards the base.

Leaf: Work from the tip towards the base.

Border: Work the double lines using a small embossing tool.

Corner pattern: Work the 'droplets' towards the tip.

Circles: Work in a small circular movement.

Perforation Fix the underside of the card accurately over the pattern and perforate using a four-pronged tool. When perforating is completed, remove the card from the pattern.

Cutting Cut the 4-hole groups to form star-shaped holes.

Cut the 8-hole groups to form the small rectangles.

Finishing Add coloured insert.

Season's Greetings

Kangaroo At Sunset

Illustrated opposite

Tracing Lightly trace the design in chalk pencil.

Painting
Working on the upper side.
Kangaroo: Brown fabric paint.
Grass-trees: Flower heads in yellow fabric paint, leaves in yellow and olive-green fabric paint, and trunks and stalk in grey fabric paint.

Working on the under side.
Landscape: Oil pastels in browns, orange, blue and yellow, are applied in stripes and blended following the instructions on page 9.

Embossing The highlights on the kangaroo, grass-tree, clouds and hills are embossed from the under side.

Finishing off Add coloured insert to enhance the sunset colours.

OPPOSITE: *Kangaroo At Sunset, Ivy-leaf Violets (page 36) and Magpie Goose (page 37)*

Ivy-leaf Violets

Illustrated on page 34

Tracing
Violets: Outlines are traced in white drawing ink.
Leaves: Outlines are traced in gold drawing ink.

Painting Working on the upper side.
Stems: Use a fine leaf green felt pen.
Leaves: Paint in leaf green fabric paint. The veins are painted in gold drawing ink after the green has dried.

Working on the under side.
Violets: The inner two-thirds of the petals and the base of the bud are painted with a deep mauve felt pen.

Embossing
Violets: The outer one-third of each petal is embossed working strokes towards the centre.
Bud: The upper one-third of the bud is embossed working towards the base.

Perforation Hold the card in place on the pattern and perforate the border from the upper side.

Finishing off Add a coloured insert.

Magpie Goose

Illustrated on page 34

Tracing

Goose: Head, neck and black wing feathers are traced using a fine black marker; beak and legs are traced with a permanent red over-head projector pen; body and white wing feathers are traced using white drawing ink. Lightly draw in the background using chalk pencil.

Painting Paint black areas in black fabric paint. Colour the red areas with red perma-nent overhead projector pen.

Embossing

Working from the upper side, emboss the under wings, and the underneath of the tail. Working from the under side, emboss the body, beak, and turned-back feathers on up-per wing and legs.

Finishing off Add coloured insert.

Index